OUTSTANDING ORK

DISCOVER BRITAIN

Outstanding Orkney

by
Robert Plant

Illustrated by Grace Plant

JOHN RITCHIE LTD
CHRISTIAN PUBLICATIONS
40 Beansburn, Kilmarnock, Scotland

ISBN-13: 978 1 910513 75 0

Copyright © 2017 by John Ritchie Ltd.
40 Beansburn, Kilmarnock, Scotland

www.ritchiechristianmedia.co.uk

Typeset by John Ritchie Ltd., Kilmarnock
Printed by Bell & Bain, Glasgow

Dedication

In memory of my father
George Arthur Plant
20th December 1923 to 8th April 2015
Who served with the Home Fleet of the Royal Navy during
World War 2 and at that time spent many days on board ship
in Scapa Flow, Orkney.

Contents

Contents

Introduction

Outstanding Orkney is the second in a series of books written especially for the younger generation who want to know more about both Great Britain and their Great Bible. It is intended that the Discover Britain series will eventually build into an exciting library of several titles. The fascinating stories are told by looking back at history or by surveying landscapes and getting close to wildlife. The writer intends the books not only to be educational but also spiritual as he points his readers to vitally important truths from the Bible, God's Word. So children, pack your cases, fasten your seat belts and get ready to go on a voyage of discovery across the exciting and interesting countries and islands that make up Great Britain.

Welcome to Orkney

Orkney, a group of around seventy islands, lies just off the north coast of Scotland. If, however, you are expecting the Orkney Islands to be a continuation of the magnificent hills and mountains of the Highlands, you might be disappointed. As you drive north from Inverness into Caithness, towards Wick and John O'Groats, you will notice the landscape flattening out, with fields replacing the mountains and glens of the lower and western highlands. This arable-type landscape is the one that is replicated in Orkney, where impressive cliffs rise hundreds of feet out of the restless sea before levelling into lush, fertile fields, ideal for raising sheep and cattle, or for growing crops.

The islands are of varying sizes, stretching a distance of over fifty miles from north to south, and nearly twenty-five miles from east to west. The population of this unique and very special place is just over twenty thousand, and only twenty of the islands are inhabited. You will never be crowded out on Orkney as in some of our big cities, and, amazingly, most of the islanders have never experienced a traffic jam, or even traffic congestion!

Locals living here call themselves *Orcadians*, not to be confused with the musical instrument, the accordion!

There are two major towns, both on the Mainland. Kirkwall, the capital, is to the east, and Stromness is in the west, but do not travel to Orkney to go on a shopping spree! Apart from a recently-arrived Tesco, the majority of shops are small, friendly, quaint and privately owned. You will not find any of the big high street stores to purchase your favourite clothes and food. What you will discover are warm and friendly local people, all willing to help you and point you in the right direction in order to make your time on the islands as exciting and interesting as possible.

The Mainland and the islands to the south form a large natural harbour over eight miles wide by six miles long. This anchorage, known as Scapa Flow, was used to great effect by the British fleet of the Royal Navy during both major world wars of the last century. Several very interesting books have been written about events that took place here and we could have filled many more pages of this volume with stories in and around Scapa Flow. We have, however, confined our accounts to just the main events which unfolded, sometimes dramatically and occasionally tragically, in these waters.

Being a group of islands, many of the tales we have chosen to relate are from the sea and involve ships of one form or another. In fact, there are so many stories from the shipping lanes around these islands that it was difficult to decide which to include and which to leave out. We trust that the ones we have chosen will give you a taste of some of the interesting events that have taken place around Orkney's stormy coastline.

So have your tickets ready and come aboard as we set sail on the sea of adventure to the Orkney Islands.

The Lost Leader's Last Day

Readers of this book will certainly not be old enough to have seen the posters that were used to recruit men into the services during the First World War. They showed the stern face of a gentleman in uniform, wearing a peaked cap and the largest moustache you ever did see. The man was always pointing a finger directly at the reader, and the slogan on the poster nearly always said, 'Your country needs you!' The face on the picture belonged to Field Marshal Horatio Herbert Kitchener, otherwise known as Lord Kitchener.

At the commencement of World War One in 1914, the Prime Minister, Herbert Asquith, made Lord Kitchener his Secretary of State for War. At this time, Kitchener was already a noted and highly-esteemed soldier, having seen action in Egypt, Sudan, India and South Africa. Now his job was to mobilise an army of volunteers large enough to help defeat the German Army. One of the ways that he went about this was with the famous poster campaign using his face and pointing finger.

World War 1 Kitchener Poster

During the war, Kitchener found himself visiting troops in many places and in several countries as he sought to encourage them and give them the benefit of his vast army experience.

In June 1916 he made the trip to the Orkney Islands in order to take a Royal Navy ship to Russia. Lord Kitchener's mission was to visit the

Russian Tsar to find ways to assist Russia in the war effort. He also wanted to strengthen Russia's determination to help the Allies in the defeat of Germany. The trip was Kitchener's own plan that involved travelling from London to Thurso on the north coast of Scotland and then, after crossing to Orkney, making a perilous journey across the North Sea, round the Norwegian coast and through the Barents Sea to Arkhangelsk in Russia.

Arriving in Scapa Flow at lunchtime on Monday, 5th June 1916, Kitchener had lunch with Admiral Jellicoe, the commander of the British Fleet, on board his flagship *Iron Duke*. Later in the afternoon, Kitchener transferred to HMS *Hampshire*, a 10,800 ton cruiser which was to take him to Russia.

All day, the wind had been blowing across the islands, gradually increasing to gale force by the time *Hampshire* sailed out of Scapa at 5:30 pm. Instead of sending *Hampshire* the usual way, around the east of the islands, Admiral Jellicoe and his staff decided that it would be safer to send the ship on a westerly course where the land would offer her a little protection from the severe north-easterly winds. Two escort ships, destroyers *Unity* and *Victor*, were charged with shadowing *Hampshire* for the first two hundred miles of her journey. By the time the lead ship reached the open sea and commenced on a northerly heading, the wind direction had changed and was now coming from the north west, directly at the three exposed ships. The sea was a furious cauldron, and the two slower and smaller escort boats struggled to keep up with the larger, more powerful *Hampshire*. Eventually, *Hampshire*'s Captain Savill ordered his two escorting ships to return to Scapa, informing them that he would go it alone on his journey to Russia.

As *Hampshire* passed Marwick Head at around 7:40 pm, the Fraser family, who owned a farm there, saw the ship ploughing through the storm about a mile out to sea. They then saw a puff of smoke, followed by a loud explosion and a flash of flame shooting from the ship into the sky. The cruiser sank within fifteen minutes. Of her crew of 749 men on board at the time, only twelve survived the sinking and the storm. Lord Kitchener – general, war secretary, soldier and national hero – was gone. His body was never recovered.

It was later discovered that a German submarine *U-75* had laid mines along the passage taken by *Hampshire* a few days before the disaster. Despite many conspiracy theories concerning the loss of the ship and its important passenger, it is pretty well recognised that it was one of these mines which was responsible for sinking her. Several days later, a British minesweeper discovered and removed a number of other mines in the area, supporting this conclusion.

In 1926, ten years after he died, the people of Orkney dedicated a memorial to Lord Kitchener in the form of a fifteen-metre-high tower. The Kitchener Memorial, as it became known, sits on the cliff tops above Marwick Head, overlooking the resting place of HMS *Hampshire* and the 737 men who died when she sank.

The Bible contains several stories of ships, boats and even shipwrecks. One day the Lord Jesus was crossing the Sea of Galilee in a small boat when a huge storm blew up, causing panic amongst the disciples who were with Him. The Lord was asleep at the stern (rear) of the boat with His head on a pillow, when the disciples in their great distress woke Him, exclaiming, '*Carest Thou not that we perish?*' Immediately the Lord Jesus stood up and, speaking to the wind and the waves, said, '*Peace, be still,*' and the Bible records there was '*a great calm.*' Such a display of power caused the disciples to ask '*What manner of man is this, that even the wind and the sea obey Him?*' It was a very good question and one that the Bible, the Word of God, answers time and time again: He is none other than the Son of God, the Saviour of the world. He can still even the fiercest storm in your life if, first of all, you are willing to trust Him as your Saviour. He offers the invitation, '*Come unto me...and I will give you rest*' (Matthew ch11v28). You can read the story of the great storm in Mark ch4v35-41.

Lifeboat Heroes of Longhope

If you live near the sea, at some time or other you will come across wonderful people who freely give up their time to volunteer for the Royal National Lifeboat Institution, the RNLI. Some of these men and women are lifeguards who patrol many of Britain's and Ireland's busy holiday beaches, giving advice about safety, and generally ensuring that everyone is kept safe. Others make up some of the many lifeboat crews which are prepared to go to the rescue of needy seamen in all weather, regardless of the risk to themselves. The RNLI saves many lives each year, from those on board sinking ships, to those who have fallen overboard into the sea, or others who may have been cut off by the tide. They also attend a host of other different emergencies. The coastlines of our country are all made safer by these great and brave people.

The islands around Orkney are no strangers to shipwreck, death and disaster and, as a result, the various lifeboat stations on the islands oftentimes tend to be kept busier than most. It was from Longhope village on the island of Hoy, where one of Orkney's lifeboats was stationed, that tragedy unfolded during the night of 17th March 1969.

On this night, a cargo ship, *Irene*, was struggling along the east side of South Ronaldsay, battling a Force 9 gale. Around 7:00 pm, she sent a distress message, asking for immediate assistance, as she was unable to cope in horrendous conditions and was starting to be pushed towards the shore. *Irene* also sent up distress rockets which were seen by some on South Ronaldsay, who immediately left their homes to watch the ship as it was driven closer to the shore by the force of the storm and the eighteen-metre-high waves.

Sometime after 7:30 pm, the Longhope lifeboat was launched, with its nine-man crew, to commence battling through the atrocious conditions in order to make the twenty-plus-mile journey and render assistance to the crew of *Irene*.

Irene ran aground at Grimness on the east side of South Ronaldsay. As local people were already waiting and prepared, they were able to fire rockets with ropes attached, and set up a breeches buoy. This is a special chair attached to ropes that can be pulled across from one side to the other, therefore evacuating the ship one person at a time.

Whilst all this was taking place, the Longhope lifeboat, strangely named the *T.G.B.*, was making slow progress through mountainous seas towards the scene. The lifeboat was spotted just after 9:00 pm off the island of Swona, and, half an hour later, just off the coast of the Cantick Head lighthouse, having travelled no more than five miles in two hours. From 10:00 pm, several attempts were made to contact the *T.G.B.* by wireless, but each was met with silence. The Kirkwall lifeboat, *Grace Paterson Ritchie*, also seeking to assist *Irene*, was asked sometime after 11:00 pm to contact the *T.G.B.* As radio transmissions were not being answered, the Kirkwall lifeboat fired a parachute flare high into the sky, expecting a response from *T.G.B.*, but no answering flare was seen. Due to the appalling weather, no search and rescue operation could begin until first light, when the Kirkwall lifeboat once again put to sea along with those from Stronsay, Thurso and Stromness. Also helping in the search was a helicopter flying out of Lossiemouth and an RAF Shackleton aircraft from RAF Kinloss.

Finally, at 1:40 pm in the afternoon, the Thurso lifeboat spotted the upturned hull of the *T.G.B.* floating some four miles south of the island of Hoy. The *T.G.B.* was taken in tow, still upside down, to Scrabster harbour at Thurso, where, in stunned silence, the bodies of seven of the eight crew were recovered from its cabin area. Amongst those who died that day were two fathers, along with their two sons. The body of one crewman, the assistant mechanic, was never recovered from the sea.

It was a tragedy that affected every home in Longhope, and just about every home in the island of Hoy, but its effect was felt around the world. Just over a year later, the Queen Mother visited Hoy to unveil a statue of a lifeboat man standing looking out to sea from the cemetery in which the bodies of the gallant heroes were laid to rest. The monument stands at the head of their graves, a fitting reminder of the ultimate sacrifice of eight gallant men.

Memorial to the crew of the Longhope Lifeboat

It is always good to remember those, perhaps our parents or our grandparents, who have sacrificed something to help us. The Lord Jesus made a very searching statement – *'Greater love hath no man than this, that a man lay down his life for his friends'* (John ch15v13). The brave and fearless lifeboat men did not know the crew of *Irene* when they launched *T.G.B.* into the howling storm. However, they were prepared to go and try to save others, and in doing so lost their own lives. The Bible records that the Lord Jesus came to *'seek and to save that which was lost'* (Luke ch19v10). He came from Heaven, knowing that He would have to die on the cross in order to save sinners like you and me. This was without doubt the greatest act of sacrifice that has ever been undertaken. Millions of people down through the years have been thankful to God that He sent His Son *'to save sinners'*(1ˢᵗ Timothy ch1v15) and make us fit for Heaven. Have you ever trusted the Lord Jesus who died to save you, and lives to keep you, as your Saviour?

The Chapel built by Captives

Could you ever imagine being taken prisoner by a foreign country and then sent to some faraway place to work for your enemy, not knowing how long you would be there or when you would be able to return to your family? That was the sad plight of over five hundred Italian prisoners captured in 1942 during the Second World War. They were transported to Orkney and placed in what became known as Camp 60, situated on the small island of Lamb Holm between the Mainland and South Ronaldsay. Here they worked on what became known as the Churchill Barriers.

In 1943, with the approval of their British captors, some of the prisoners commenced a project to create a small chapel for a place of worship for the mostly Roman Catholic prisoners. Two corrugated Nissen huts were acquired and joined together end to end. Using leftover concrete from the construction of the barriers, they created a frontage to make it look like a real church, as well as making and shaping the altar and altar rail. Others used plasterboard to line the interior and then painted it, whilst Domenico Chiocchetti set about intricately painting what became known as the sanctuary. The prisoners were very creative, using a variety of objects to help give the chapel the appearance of a real church building. They used corned beef tins as candle holders, and a car exhaust, covered in concrete, was made into the font. After two years of painstaking work and intricate detail, the chapel was completed, along with incredible artwork by Chiocchetti.

Italian Chapel

After the conclusion of the war in 1945, the prisoners were returned to Italy, but many years later some revisited Orkney in order to see the chapel they had created. In 1960, Chiocchetti came back with a mission – to restore the neglected chapel to its former pristine condition, which he did, working hard in the little building he had helped to create during the harsh years of war. The chapel now stands as a monument to those Italian prisoners who, despite being held as prisoners of war, still sought somehow to find a place to worship God.

Despite all the amazing efforts of these prisoners, the Bible actually tells us that *'God that made the world and all things therein, seeing that He is Lord of Heaven and earth, dwelleth not in temples made with hands'* (Acts ch17v24). God is accessible to anyone who really seeks Him, for He says, *'Ye shall seek Me, and find Me, when ye shall search for Me with all your heart.'* (Jeremiah ch29v13). Today, the work of the Italian chapel still stands as a monument to the determination and dedication of those hardy Italian prisoners. However, the soul that seeks God and finds Him by trusting His Son, the Lord Jesus, as Saviour, will become a monument to God's great salvation as he rejoices in Heaven throughout all eternity.

The Do or Die Mission

As the First World War drew to its final inevitable close, the German Navy decided to attempt one last daring attack on the British fleet in their home port of Scapa Flow. The attack was to show that, despite losing the war, the German Navy was still a force to be reckoned with. It was also anticipated that if the raid was successful it would instil some pride back into the defeated German nation. It was the Germans' final 'do or die' mission.

The newly-commissioned 519-ton submarine, *UB116*, set sail from Heligoland on 25th October 1918 with a crew of thirty-seven, and eleven torpedoes. The orders had been given to enter Scapa Flow and sink as many British ships as possible, regardless of the risk. Unfortunately for the German Navy and the submarine's crew, intelligence provided to the German fleet was not up to date. Scapa Flow had been more or less cleared of British shipping in the run up to the soon-anticipated German surrender.

The captain of *UB116*, Lieutenant J J Emsmann, had been instructed to enter Scapa Flow through the Hoxa Sound entrance. German observations had noted that this approach was regularly used by British ships and it was thereby deduced that no defences were in operation. How wrong they were! Hoxa Sound was guarded by an elaborate minefield, cable detector loops and hydrophones that could pick up the sound of any approaching shipping.

On the evening of 28th October 1918, *UB116* approached Hoxa Sound on its deadly mission to enter the Flow. At 8:21 pm, the hydrophones picked up the sound of approaching engines. No British ships were expected that night, so those manning the extensive defence systems came to full alert. Three hours later, *UB116*'s periscope was spotted as the submarine continued to make its stealthy way towards its target. A few minutes later, the detector loops picked up the submarine's presence, sending the galvanometer in the shore-based operations room at Flotta frantic. The submarine was approaching the deadly minefield, located on the seabed. The mines were detonated and the German Navy's final attempt to inflict damage on the Royal Navy was over. The subsequent explosion destroyed the submarine in an instant and claimed the lives of all thirty-seven unfortunate crew members. The following day, divers sent down to examine the wrecked submarine were met with the gruesome sight of the fragmented hull torn open like a tin can. Bodies and body parts were scattered throughout the accessible hull. One can only imagine how awful the last seconds of these men's lives must have been.

War is always a dreadful thing and, sadly, many innocent people end up suffering its consequences. The Bible, however, states that 'the eyes of the wicked shall fail, and they shall not escape, and their hope shall be as the giving up of the ghost' (Job ch11v20). Just as the various British warning and protection systems picked up the presence of German submarine UB116, so God sees everything that goes on in the world, and sinners 'shall not escape' unless they turn to the Lord Jesus who died to save them. Once again, the Bible warns, 'How shall we escape, if we neglect so great salvation?' (Hebrews ch2v3) The answer is simple – the only escape from sin and its eternal consequences in Hell is to rest on who the Lord Jesus is and what He has done on the cross.

The Valiant Viking

As you walk through the small town of Kirkwall, Orkney's capital, there is one building that completely dominates the landscape from whichever direction you look. This marvellous building is the large, impressive, red-stoned St Magnus Cathedral. The cathedral was commenced in 1137AD, around twenty years after the death of Magnus himself, and was constructed by Magnus's nephew Rognvald.

St Magnus Cathedral

So just who was St Magnus and whatever did he do to warrant the construction of the largest and most majestic building in Orkney? Magnus Erlendsson was born in 1080. His father, Erlend, ruled Orkney jointly along with his brother Paul. In 1098, another Magnus (Magnus Barelegs) arrived from Norway and overthrew Magnus's father and uncle, banishing them to Norway where they both soon died. Magnus Barelegs then set up his son Sigurd as king of Orkney. Are you with me so far?

Magnus Barelegs then went on a raiding spree along the western coast of Scotland, ensuring that he took Magnus and his cousin Haakon (Uncle Paul's son) with him, possibly to ensure that they did not cause his own son Sigurd any bother in Orkney.

Having sailed as far south as North Wales, King Magnus Barelegs set about attacking the rulers of Anglesey. When asked to join the fighting, Magnus is alleged to have said, "I have no quarrel with them!" Instead of fighting, he stayed on board his ship, playing his harp and singing hymns, much to the annoyance of King Magnus Barelegs. Realising that the king would most probably put him to death for cowardice, Magnus decided to escape from the ship one night as it was returning to Scotland and swam safely to the Scottish shore. Magnus went into hiding in Scotland until he heard of the death of King Magnus Barelegs in Ireland in 1102.

In 1105, Magnus returned to Orkney where his cousin Haakon had become Earl after Sigurd had returned to jointly rule Norway. Magnus was granted permission to rule jointly with his cousin, and this he did until 1114, when trouble struck.

At some period, and as a result of the interference of others, the two cousins quarrelled to such an extent that war was declared between the two men. Thankfully, battle was averted through the help of neutral counsellors and a treaty of peace was prepared. This was to be finally agreed at a meeting between Haakon and Magnus on the Isle of Egilsay.

Magnus arrived first, but upon seeing Haakon approaching with a fleet of eight warships he knew that he had been betrayed. After hiding that night, Magnus was captured and brought before Haakon and a group of island chieftains. It was clear that joint rule between the two cousins was no longer an option.

Magnus offered to go on a pilgrimage and never return to Orkney, or be exiled and imprisoned in Scotland. These two suggestions were both rejected. Finally, he suggested to his cousin that "you mutilate me in any way you choose or else blind me and lock me in a dungeon." It seems that this idea gained Haakon's approval but not that of the chieftains of the islands also gathered with him who were determined to end the dual rule. They wanted to put to death one of their leaders, but which of the two cousins should die?

Haakon argued that he enjoyed ruling the Orkney Islands and was not prepared to die. Magnus made no representation for himself, and having comforted his followers, he stepped forward, ready to die. Haakon did not find executing Magnus as easy as he had thought, as his standard bearer angrily refused to carry out his command to kill the kindly Magnus. Eventually, Haakon's cook, Lifolf, was ordered to perform the gruesome act, and after being forgiven by Magnus for the act he was about to carry out, with tears streaming down his face, he swung the axe and split Magnus' head in two.

After being buried initially where he died, the body of Magnus was removed and reburied in Birsay. During renovation work of the cathedral in 1919, a box was discovered containing various bones, including a badly-severed skull. Experts examining the find concluded that they had found the remains of Magnus.

The story of Magnus willingly dying in order to give life to another easily reminds us of the work of the Lord Jesus on the cross. The apostle Paul wrote about it – 'The Son of God who loved me and gave Himself for me' (Galatians ch2v20). The Lord Jesus willingly died that we might have eternal life through Him. Thankfully, though, three days later He rose from the dead and now lives in Heaven, ready to 'save them to the uttermost that come unto God by Him' (Hebrews ch7v25).

Vole in a Hole

As long as you are an animal lover and not afraid of mice, you will adore the wee vole. The vole is a cousin of the mouse, but is different in many ways. It looks fatter, is shorter in length and has a short, hairy tail. The mouse has a distinct neck, but the head of the vole looks like it is part of the body. The vole is certainly much cuter than the mouse!

All in all, there are about 155 species of vole across the world, ranging in size from around seven to twenty centimetres. If you are fortunate enough to see one, take a good, hard look at the little chap, as it has a very short life expectancy, usually not more than six months and certainly never more than a year. Sadly, the mortality rate of new-born voles is remarkably high, with over 80% dying within the first month of life. They are, however, very productive breeders and a female can produce around ten litters of ten babies during her lifetime, resulting in one hundred offspring in less than a year.

Voles are experts at burrowing and can produce an impressive and extensive system of tunnels very quickly. Unfortunately, they like to eat succulent plant roots and especially bulbs, the results often not being seen until the plant dies or the bulbs fail to germinate as usual.

The Orkney Vole

It was in 1805 that the minister of Shapinsay noticed that the voles he could see on the island were slightly different to the usual European species. What has become known as the Orkney vole is slightly larger than its counterpart found throughout the rest of the British Isles, and for years the question of its origin has caused confusion among naturalists. Voles, unlike rats, are not good sailors and will usually take great pains to avoid ships. It has been suggested that the Orkney vole came in one of the ships of the Spanish Armada, which was wrecked on the islands in 1588. Remains of voles discovered in Skara Brae apparently date back over four thousand years. It would seem that this unusual little rodent originated in the areas of southern France or northern Spain.

Sadly, as most voles are rather shy creatures, you are not too likely to come across one unless you can discover a run issuing from a nest site. If you do, sit tight downwind and wait in the hope of catching a small glimpse as it runs past you through the long grass, going about its everyday business.

The Orkney vole is rare enough even in the Orkneys so you need to know in which islands to find it. It will only be discovered on the Mainland, Sanday, Westray, Rousay and South Ronaldsay. Happy hunting!

Wildlife is a wonderful testimony to the fact that every mammal, bird and fish has a designer and creator behind it. When people design something, it is usually a copy of something already seen in nature. From the millions of differing stars in the sky to the incredible creatures that live hidden hundreds of metres under the sea, it is easy to see that God is a great God of variety. No wonder the Psalmist could exclaim, 'When I consider Thy heavens, the work of Thy fingers, the moon and the stars, which Thou hast ordained; what is man?' (Psalm 8v3&4) The creation of God is so extensive, and even the humble Orkney vole gives witness to its Creator.

Terror by Night

Friday, 13th October 1939, was a day just like any other for the sailors on board HMS *Royal Oak* at anchor in the relative safety of Scapa Flow. However, little did anyone know that before the sun had risen the next day, 833 of the ship's crew would have died in the freezing waters, the victims of a daring German U-boat (submarine) attack.

Although *Royal Oak* was twenty-five years old, she was still a formidable and impressive ship. Costing over two million pounds, she was one of Britain's largest battleships of the time, measuring 190 metres long and weighing around thirty thousand tons.

That night, just six weeks after war had been declared, a German submarine named *U-47*, commanded by Captain Günther Prien, was making a daring attempt to gain access to Scapa Flow in order to attack any British ships at anchor there. Carefully navigating his submarine through the Kirk Sound between the island of Lamb Holm and Orkney Mainland, as well as past a series of blockships (ships that had been positioned and sunk to stop access to the Flow), Prien found himself within the confines of the British anchorage of Scapa Flow.

Sometime earlier, the British had observed a German photographic reconnaissance plane. They guessed that an attack might be made and moved the majority of its large ships out of the Flow. Prien sailed into a surprisingly empty anchorage and struggled to find any targets at all. As he turned back on himself, his lookout spotted *Royal Oak* at anchor about four thousand metres away.

HMS Royal Oak

Prien ordered his crew to attack and, just before 1:00 am, fired off a salvo of three torpedoes in the direction of the British ship. Two missed their target, but the third hit the bow of the giant ship and exploded, waking up the majority of the crew who had been asleep in their hammocks. The sailors initially thought that a small explosion had taken place in the ship's forward store where paint and other inflammable liquids were kept. No one suspected that they were under attack from an enemy submarine hidden in the darkness of Scapa Flow, its captain watching carefully their every move.

Ten minutes later, Captain Prien fired another torpedo from his stern tubes, aiming for HMS *Pegasus*, a seaplane transport ship. However, this also missed its target. Taking time to carefully align himself, Prien once again used his forward tubes to send another three torpedoes on their way through the cold, dark sea towards their target. This time, two of the three struck *Royal Oak* amidships (right in the middle) and exploded, tearing a massive hole in the ship's starboard (right) side.

The exploding torpedoes then ignited other explosive substances on board the ship, and a massive fireball ripped through *Royal Oak*, frying men where they lay in their hammocks. The ship began to roll over and sink. Many sailors jumped into the freezing waters, wearing only their night clothes. Within fifteen minutes of *U-47*'s second strike, *Royal Oak* had completely turned over and sunk to the bottom of Scapa Flow.

As soon as Prien and his crew heard and saw the explosion, they made good their escape at full speed, once again negotiating the blockships between Lamb Holm and the Mainland. Within an hour of making its first attack, U-47 and her crew were in the relative safety of the North Sea and steering for home.

Meanwhile, back in Scapa Flow, the devastating results of the submarine attack were becoming increasingly apparent. Hundreds of men who had managed to escape the burning, sinking hulk fought frantically to remain alive in the ice-cold waters. This was a task made almost impossible by a thick blanket of oil now covering the area, which had spilled from the stricken ship.

Mercifully, a small tender craft, Daisy 2, had been moored alongside Royal Oak. On hearing the first torpedo strike, her captain, John Gatt, suspected that more than just exploding inflammables aboard the battleship had been responsible for the explosion. He was in the wheelhouse of Daisy 2, having already made her ready for action, when the final two torpedoes struck Royal Oak. As the battleship began to keel over, it pulled Daisy 2 right out of the water by the attached ropes. Captain Gatt immediately had some of these connecting hawsers cut. Others broke under the strain, allowing Daisy 2 to fall back into the sea and commence rescuing survivors from the sinking vessel. During the night, the drifter picked up 386 men, at one point becoming so overcrowded that she herself was in danger of sinking. As day dawned, it sadly became obvious that no more survivors were going to be found.

On 20th October, Winston Churchill, at that time First Lord of the Admiralty, made a statement in the House of Commons, acknowledging that Günther Prien's actions in U-47 were 'a remarkable exploit of professional skill and daring.'

On his return to Germany, Prien and his crew of forty were feted as celebrities and personally rewarded by Adolf Hitler, the German leader. Captain Prien was nicknamed 'The Bull of Scapa Flow'. In total, Prien was responsible for the sinking of over thirty allied ships during his short career. However, even Captain Prien did not survive the war, for he and his crew on board U-47 were lost in action on 7th March 1941.

How important it is as Christians to be ever aware of the danger that is all around us, which can creep up and catch us out just when we least expect it. The Bible speaks of the devil acting like an *'angel of light'* (2nd Corinthians ch11v14) and, as such, he can make things appear to be quite harmless and fun, when underneath there is great danger. The apostle Paul, writing about the devil, explained that *'we are not ignorant of his devices'* (2nd Corinthians ch2v11), and therefore we should always be on the alert to danger that could catch us unawares and drag us and our testimony down.

Churchill's Connecting and Protecting Barriers

After the sinking of the Royal Oak in 1939, and with it the proven fact that enemy submarines could enter Scapa Flow, plans were hastily put in place to block the eastern approaches to the Flow. This was, in fact, not a new idea, as plans to link South Ronaldsay with the Mainland had been discussed before World War One. With the loss of a ship the size of Royal Oak, along with over eight hundred men, these plans now belatedly became a reality.

Winston Churchill, who months later was to become the British Prime Minister, was First Lord of the Admiralty and therefore responsible for the safety of the Royal Navy whilst at anchor. He gave permission for construction of four causeways to be built, linking the Orkney Mainland with South Ronaldsay via the smaller islands of Burray, Lamb Holm and Glims Holm.

Building work began immediately, and a disused passenger liner initially provided accommodation for some of the 1,700 men involved in the massive undertaking. Overhead cableways were erected to drop the required rocks and blocks into position. In order to hold some of the smaller rocks in place, giant wire nets were created and filled with locally-quarried stone. It has been estimated that these nets contained in excess of a quarter of a million tonnes of differing shaped and sized rocks. In addition, nearly seventy thousand five- and ten-tonne concrete blocks were also produced at the site, the small blocks making up the centre of the causeway, whilst the larger ten-tonne concrete cubes were placed along the sides in order to act as wave breaks against the strong tides.

At first, progress was slow due to poor weather, lack of materials and workers, and the fast-flowing tides that raced in between the islands. In 1942, Italian prisoners of war arrived and were put to work, helping to complete the mammoth project. Initially, the prisoners complained that, as the barriers were to keep enemy ships and submarines out of Scapa Flow, they were not allowed to undertake the work in accordance with an international agreement called the Geneva Convention. Eventually, after much discussion and debate, it was put to them that the causeways were 'improvements to communications to the southern Orkney Islands.' On hearing this, the prisoners, realising that the causeways would indeed assist local people by connecting the islands together, dropped their objections and set to work.

The project was massive, even by today's standards, and took five years to complete. It was officially opened on 12th May 1945, four days after World War Two had ended. The cost was well in excess of two million pounds. However, the benefits to the islands that the causeways connected and brought together have been felt and appreciated ever since.

The Churchill Barriers causeway has indeed made a difference to the local Orcadians, especially those living on South Ronaldsay, who, since their completion, have been able to drive to Kirkwall instead of taking a ferry. Thankfully, a connection has been made for us to Heaven that had been broken as a result of sin. The Word of God states that 'there is one God, and one mediator (link) between God and men, the man Christ Jesus; who gave Himself a ransom for all' (1st Timothy ch2v5&6). In order to bring a sinless God and sinful people together, the Lord Jesus came to earth, lived a pure, sinless life and willingly died to bring eternal life to all who trust Him as Saviour.

Old-Style Living

Skara Brae is what is known as a Neolithic village. It dates from around 2500BC, so its history goes back before the time of the Lord. It has been suggested that the village was originally buried and therefore preserved by a sandstorm sometime before 2000BC. Remarkably, it was another storm, during the 1800s, that, as the result of extremely high tides, fully revealed this remarkable archaeological find.

Skara Brae, or 'The Brae' to local Orcadians, is a small collection of seven houses, all interconnected by passages. The houses are so well preserved that it is possible to see beds, fireplaces, dressers and cupboards, all built into the various walls. It is fascinating to walk around this wonderful piece of history and try to imagine what life would have been like for the inhabitants about one thousand years after creation. Remarkably, once the house was excavated completely, it was observed that the original builders had used blue clay along the bottom layer of brickwork to work as a damp course. This was a great discovery and experts suggest that the blue clay would have worked just as well in keeping the house dry as today's damp courses made mostly of polythene.

The Lord Jesus, in one of His parables, told the story of two men who set about building their houses. The story is found in Matthew ch7v24-27. One man built using a rock foundation and discovered that, even in a great storm, his house stood firm. The other sadly built on the sand and found, to his cost, that when the storm arrived, his house collapsed around him. If we are saved, we have a good foundation, *'Jesus Christ Himself being the chief corner stone'* (Ephesians ch2v20). Once we are saved, we can never be lost. God, however, expects us to make progress as Christians in living for and being pleasing to Him. There are many ways to do this but two foundational verses, found in Acts chapter 2 provide some excellent advice. *'Then they that gladly received his word were baptized: and the same day there were added unto them about three thousand souls. And they continued stedfastly in the apostles' doctrine and fellowship, and in breaking of bread, and in prayers'* (v41-42). If we are Christians, we will desire to be baptised (in the biblical way by being completely immersed in water) and join a company of other Christians who meet regularly to worship God and learn from His Word.

The roofs of the houses, although no longer in existence, were possibly supported by whale bones. Suggestions have been made that, as whales were far more common in those days, if one was stranded it could have provided all the roof supports required in Skara Brae as well as oil and other useful items for the inhabitants.

One of the buildings excavated, simply called Hut 8, seems to have been a workshop where a kiln had been built, possibly to dry the various pots that were also discovered. The kiln may also have played a part in drying the various meagre crops the inhabitants grew. Unfortunately, the surrounding peat bog was not good for preserving any of the wooden items from the area, so sadly many of these have been lost. Despite this, many other items have been discovered, such as pots, carved stones, pins produced by filing down bones to a point, and jewellery made from various small or shaped bones and animal teeth.

A visit to Skara Brae at any time is an education, allowing you to discover just how people lived on the islands thousands of years ago, as well as to show just how civilised they really were.

Flight into History

Today, if you were to join a conversation about warships of any type, eventually someone would make mention of aircraft carriers. These gigantic ships cost millions of pounds to build, help to protect our islands and played a huge part in the Second World War. They commenced life, however, as a result of trials held around the Orkney Islands in August 1917.

During its construction in Wallsend, near Newcastle, the battlecruiser HMS *Furious* was selected to have major modifications made in order for it to become the world's first aircraft carrier – the forerunner of all that would follow. Once complete, the ship was brought into service in June 1917. Unfortunately, despite being built as an aircraft carrier, design changes had been made too late, and aircraft attempting to land on the ship had to avoid crashing into the ship's bridge and upper metal works before putting down on a very short runway. It was by no means an easy task to land an aircraft safely on the deck of *Furious*!

On board the ship, as it sailed around the Orkney Islands in 1917, were five twin-winged Sopwith Pup aircraft. It was one of these fragile-looking planes in which Squadron Commander Ernest Dunning of the Royal Navy Air Service was going to attempt to become the first person in the world to land on a moving ship at sea.

Dunning had several practices, flying up behind the ship and manoeuvring his plane into position for a landing during perfect conditions during July, but without attaining his goal – an actual landing.

On 2nd August, with HMS *Furious* sailing into a 21 knot (25mph) headwind and travelling at a rather fast 26 knots (29mph), Commander Dunning fought to bring his aircraft into position for a landing. As he slowed up in the wind, his plane seemed to remain stationary over the ship. The watching group of sailors and officers ran onto the deck

Ernest Dunning lands his Sopwith Pup aircraft

and, reaching up, grabbed Dunning's plane, ignominiously pulling it down onto the ship's runway. The first landing of an aircraft upon a moving ship at sea had been accomplished, although in a somewhat unorthodox manner!

Five days later, on 7th August, Dunning again repeated the feat, this time without having to be finally pulled down onto the deck. He took off and attempted his third landing on a moving ship at sea. Trying to avoid all the various dangers on the deck was not easy for the gallant and daring pilot. Unfortunately, as he came in once again his right wheel clipped the rim of the landing deck and went over the edge, tipping the aircraft off the ship's runway and over the side into the sea. Even in August, the waters around the Orkney Islands are very cold, and despite the heroic attempts of those on board the ship to rescue the stricken pilot, their attempts were in vain, as he had drowned by the time help reached him.

Commander Dunning's loss was keenly felt, but what he had accomplished before his last ill-fated attempt proved that aircraft could land and take off from ships whilst at sea and paved the way for modern aircraft carriers of the world. A year later, in 1918, the world's first purpose-built aircraft carrier with a full-length runway, HMS Argus was launched, almost as if in recognition of the dead pilot's ground-breaking attainment.

In 1992, to mark the 75th anniversary of what Squadron Commander Ernest Dunning accomplished in 1917, a permanent memorial was erected at Smoogro on the shores of Scapa Flow in recognition of his outstanding contribution to the use of aircraft at sea.

The Bible speaks of the Lord Jesus as the 'forerunner' – 'Which hope we have as an anchor of the soul, both sure and stedfast, and which entereth into that within the veil; whither the forerunner is for us entered, even Jesus' (Hebrews ch6v19&20). A forerunner is someone who goes before, someone who leads the way. Commander Ernest Dunning led the way (was a forerunner) in landing on a ship. The Bible, however, tells us that the Lord Jesus leads the way into Heaven, and as a result is like the anchor on a ship that holds it still and steady in the midst of the storm. So when we turn from our sin and trust the Lord Jesus as Saviour, He becomes to us like an anchor linking us to Heaven, where He has already gone, awaiting our arrival. What a glorious forerunner He became, and what a strong anchor He is to those of us who are saved.

A Variety of Vikings

Have you ever complained about your name? Perhaps you wish your parents had given you a different one, especially if it is rather unusual. Well, if you have ever thought that way, stop and consider these Viking men and their rather amazing names.

Harald Fairhair

Harald was the first king of Norway and reigned for fifty-eight years, although there is no record of his hair colour. Unfortunately, it seems that Harald made many enemies during his reign, often chasing them out of Norway. Some of those who left ended up living in the Orkney Islands. Harald, however, was still fearful of their power and so arranged an expedition to the west, visiting Iceland, Shetland, Faroe and Orkney in order to deal once and for all with those whom he considered opposed to him.

Eric Bloodaxe

Eric was Harald's son and, despite his bloodthirsty name, it does not seem that he went about swinging his axe. He did, however, become not only King of Norway but also conquered the north of England to become King of Northumbria. Several stories relate his visits to the Orkney Islands during his various reigns.

Harald Smooth-tongue

Not too much is recorded about Harald Smooth-tongue, other than the fact that he was Earl of Orkney for about five years, eventually dying on Christmas Day 1131, aged around 27. He was also known as Harald 'The Orator', and as both his nicknames have a speech connection, it seems that perhaps that he was good at talking.

The Bible gives some sound advice when it states *'See that ye refuse not Him that speaketh'* (Hebrews ch12v25). Today, God does not speak with a great booming voice that shakes the earth, but simply through His Word, the Bible. It is vitally important that we read it in order to understand what God's will is for our lives. In reading the Bible, we will discover that it has a cleansing effect upon our lives and it will help to keep us away from sin and free from harm, because *'every word of God is pure: He is a shield unto them that put their trust in Him'* (Proverbs ch30v5).

Thorstein Clumsymouth

There really is very little written about this poor character in history. Perhaps that is because his name says it all. Was he one of those people who often disengage their brain before saying something?

ThorfinnTorf- Einarsson Skull-splitter

Here is yet another interesting character of which little is actually recorded. He was the third generation Earl of Orkney and had five sons who all succeeded him in various forms as rulers of either Orkney or nearby Caithness on the northern tip of Scotland. Thankfully, there are no accounts of him living up to his murderous name.

Magnus Barelegs

We have already met this interesting character in our chapter about St

Magnus. However, is it just possible that Magnus was the first Viking to adopt the kilt as his usual form of attire?

Olaf the White

Olaf was born in Ireland and became King of Dublin around 853BC. His wife, Aud the Deep-minded, was a daughter of the King of the Hebrides and, as a result of this Scottish connection, Olaf had a deep interest in Scotland and its islands, especially Orkney. This could explain his son Thorstein's desire to rule over the land.

Thorstein the Red

Thorstein was the son of Olaf the White. Although born in Dublin, he left and moved up to the Hebridean Islands off Scotland's west coast. It is obvious that his new home did not provide him with the action that he craved, so he sailed to the Scottish mainland to become a warlord, eventually conquering half of Scotland and demanding taxes from his new subjects. Sadly for Thorstein, some Scottish clansmen rebelled against his rule and had him killed. The 'red' in his name could come from his love for fighting and killing people, thus spilling their blood, or it could possibly be a reminder of his own violent death at the hands of those he sought to conquer.

William the Old

William was Bishop of Orkney during the 1100s. One source states that he held this position for sixty-six years, this longevity possibly being the reason for his unusual name. It was through much of William's effort that St Magnus Cathedral was built in Kirkwall.

Thorfinn the Mighty

A local Orkney account of Thorfinn describes him as 'unusually tall and strong, an ugly-looking man with a black head of hair, sharp features, a big nose and bushy eyebrows, a forceful man, greedy for fame and fortune. He did well in battle, for he was both a good tactician and full of courage.' I wonder how someone might describe you? It would appear that Thorfinn was ruler of most of the Scottish islands as well as the Isle of Man during his life.

The Big Game

No, it is not football or rugby. It is not even something associated with the Highland games. Welcome to the wonderful world of the Ba'! It is really quite difficult to describe Ba' as it is almost a cross between football and rugby. The ball is round, like a football, but can be (and usually is) held and thrown like a rugby ball. Ba' is played twice a year, New Year's Day and Christmas Day, by hundreds of people along the streets of Kirkwall. So large and involved are the crowds that come to take part, that shops and other premises along the route of the game board up their doors and windows to protect them from the press of people as they pass by whilst taking part in the game.

The same two teams compete each year, the Uppies and the Doonies, although the correct names for the teams are 'Up the Gates', and 'Down the Gates'. The Ba' is actually the name of the ball that is used, which is slightly smaller than a football. The starting place is the Market Cross outside St Magnus Cathedral, and kick-off time is always 1:00 pm. Once the action commences, the Ba' can disappear into the scrum of hands for quite a long time before suddenly popping up from the crowd and over the heads of the players. Occasionally, someone can break free from the crowd and make a charge towards the opponents' goal, gaining many metres for their team.

The Ba'

The Ba's goals must be some of the most unusual anywhere in sport. The Doonies' is the sea somewhere around Kirkwall Harbour, and the Uppies' is the wall on the corner of Main Street and New Scapa Road, so there are no posts or nets involved in this strange game.

The harbour town of Stromness also followed the capital, Kirkwall, in organising a Ba' game during the latter part of the 1880s, but, for whatever reason, the council ruled the game had to be stopped and this duly occurred in 1924. There was, however, another equally strange and different game played in Stromness, called simply The Yule Tree! This rather unusual game involved cutting down some unsuspecting person's tree on Christmas Eve and, as a result of attaching ropes to it, using it to play a sort of tug-of-war around the streets of the town. This game appears to have been more successful in Stromness than the Ba' as it lasted until 1936.

The writers of the New Testament often used sporting illustrations as they sought to encourage God's people who were being persecuted, or to explain some aspect of God's truth. The writer to the Hebrews wrote about running a marathon (Hebrews ch12v1&2). The apostle Paul often wrote of sporting participation, using the examples of an athlete (2nd Timothy ch2v5), a wrestler (2nd Timothy ch4v7) and a runner (Philippians ch3v13&14). There is one statement that Paul makes that seems to stand out above all else, which is, *'that I may win Christ'* (Philippians ch3v8). In simple language, the apostle was explaining that all else was a waste of time, except getting to (winning) Christ. The Bible really does show that this is the real priority in life because our eternal happiness depends on it.

The Stones and the Bones

If you travel to almost the centre of Orkney Mainland, halfway between Kirkwall and Stromness, you will come to Stenness, home to some rather unusual stones. These 'standing' stones were originally made up of twelve tall, thin stones arranged in a circle, but today only four remain for visitors to see. The stones were set up before the time of Christ, and are apparently older than England's famous Stonehenge. They most certainly had pagan (false religious) associations. The tallest stone still standing is over five metres high and is appropriately called the Watchstone. When careful observations are made of the sunrise and sunsets from this stone, certain important dates of pagan festivals can be determined. One stone that has been long destroyed was the Odin Stone, which was rather unique because it had a hole right through the middle of it. Courting couples could link hands via this hole and confess to each other their undying love. Apparently, despite the stone's ability to bring happiness to those in love, it was knocked down and broken up by a farmer in 1814 because he did not like people tramping across his land to pledge their love to one another!

Around the Stenness site, bones of various animals, such as cows, sheep, dogs and even the occasional human have been discovered. Maybe this was a burying site for animals and people that had died, or perhaps it was a place of sacrifice for those seeking to get right with God.

Standing Stones at Stenness

Not too far from here, you will come to another similar but far larger stone circle called The Ring of Brodgar. It has been estimated that, when it was originally set up, there may have been around sixty stones in the circle, with a diameter of over one hundred metres, twice that of the Stenness stones. Today, only twenty-seven stones remain, the tallest of which is just under five metres high. Interestingly, there is one stone that stands off by itself from the rest of the circle which has been named the Comet Stone. It has been suggested that this was set up as a place to stand in order to watch the sun setting over the Ring of Brodgar.

Both sets of stones have large ditches (or moats) surrounding them that must have taken months or even years to dig out and complete.

Whatever the strange reason for these sets of curious stones, we must confess that there is a lot of history surrounding them.

Thankfully, today we do not require stones or stone circles and sacrifices to get right with God. The Bible speaks of the Lord Jesus that He made 'one sacrifice for sins for ever' (Hebrews ch10v12), and therefore there is nothing at all that people can do to earn a place in Heaven. The Bible says that salvation is 'not of works, lest any man should boast' (Ephesians ch2v9). When the Lord Jesus died on the cross, He exclaimed, 'It is finished' (John ch19v30), and He meant just what He said. Now all He expects us to do is come into the good of His work by faith in Him.

The Poet that Wrote It

If you are anything like the writer of this book, you will love reading and will have favourite books written by your favourite authors. When I was young, I loved to read the 'Famous Five' books by Enid Blyton, or better still, the 'Biggles' books by Captain W E Johns. At some time in our lives we will follow favourite authors. If you ask Orcadians to name their favourite writers, it will not be too long before one name stands out from all the rest – George Mackay Brown.

It is often interesting to see how early events shaped the future lives of certain people. If George Mackay Brown had never contracted the terrible disease of tuberculosis in early life, he might never have turned to writing. However, this illness and its subsequent results in his life led him to work for the *Orkney Herald* newspaper and he never looked back! He was the youngest of six children, and when his father had to stop work as the local postman as a result of illness, Mackay Brown and his siblings found life hard, growing up almost in poverty.

After spending time at the University in Edinburgh, the budding poet moved back to his beloved Orkney Islands and set to work using his obvious gift to produce word pictures through his poems and stories. His writings were many and diverse. In his lifetime he produced over thirty published books of poems, children's stories, plays and novels. Mackay Brown was a true Orcadian, travelling away from his home in Stromness very infrequently and usually only across to mainland Scotland. Reading over his literary fruitful life is almost like reading one of his more sombre and sad poems. He never married or seemed to find the lady of his dreams, despite several attempts.

His description of his home islands is very short but extremely accurate – 'The essence of Orkney's magic is silence, loneliness and the deep marvellous rhythms of sea and land, darkness and light.'

Mackay Brown's poems did not necessarily rhyme as perhaps other poems do. He tended to tell stories in his writings, with each verse almost a mini tale in itself. Have a read of some verses of his classic 'Hamnavoe Market' and see if you can guess what is happening each verse.

They drove to the Market with ringing pockets.

Johnston stood beside the barrel.
All day he stood there.

He woke in a ditch, his mouth full of ashes.

Grieve bought a balloon and a goldfish.

He swung through the air.

He fired shotguns, rolled pennies, ate sweet fog from a stick.

Heddle was at the Market also.

I know nothing of his activities.

He is and always was a quiet man.

A gypsy saw in the hand of Halcro

Great strolling herds, harvests, a proud woman.

He wintered in the poorhouse.

They drove home from the Market under the stars

Except for Johnston

Who lay in a ditch, his mouth full of dying fires.

Hamnavoe was the Viking name of his hometown of Stromness and so this poem depicts a group of people who spend all day at the market in his town. Did you manage to work out what each person was doing? Let me explain.

Sadly, Johnston was getting drunk by drinking from a barrel. Grieve was having fun at all the fairground activities. No one knew what Heddle got up to, and Halcro had his fortune told by a gypsy, but, as you would expect, it did not come true.

George Mackay Brown passed away in 1996, aged 74, and is buried in his hometown of Stromness.

David, who we read about in the Bible, was a king, but it is for his great poetical works, which are preserved for us in the book of Psalms in the Word of God, that He is maybe best remembered. David wrote about very many subjects, but always with a view to getting the reader to understand and appreciate something of the greatness and goodness of God. The best known of David's writings is Psalm 23, which is often quoted at funeral services. Here, David starts by stating, *'The Lord is my shepherd; I shall not want'*, and concludes by affirming, *'I will dwell in the house of the Lord for ever'* (Psalm 23v1&6). If we have trusted the Lord Jesus as our Saviour He will guide us, like a shepherd, and we can be absolutely sure that one day we will dwell in the house of the Lord (Heaven) forever.

That Sinking Feeling

Can you imagine going out on a small boat during a school trip in order to see the ships of the defeated enemy after a major war? Then try to think what it would be like if fifty-two of those great ships suddenly started to sink all at the same time! This was the amazing spectacle that actually greeted a group of children on 21st June 1919.

In November 1918, Germany had surrendered, bringing to an end the First World War. Later that month, seventy-four German ships, along with their crews, were brought to Scapa Flow to be held whilst ongoing negotiations were underway as to how and when the sailors should be returned to Germany and what should become of their ships. Many of the original crews aboard the ships had already been returned to Germany, leaving only about five thousand men stationed on them from the original complement of around twenty thousand.

German Rear-Admiral Ludwig Von Reuter was greatly concerned about the outcome of negotiations taking place in Paris concerning the fate of his ships. He was certain that they would all be handed over into the hands of the victorious allied forces, notably, Britain, France and Italy. Von Reuter was convinced that such actions would bring lasting shame upon the German Navy, its officers and crews, so he made plans for the German crews still aboard the seventy-four captured ships to sink them at a given command from himself.

At 11:20 am, the day the peace treaty was to be signed in Paris, Rear-Admiral Von Reuter gave the command to scuttle (sink) the ships. The German crews had already made plans for such an operation, ensuring that portholes, watertight doors and hatches were left open. Some had even drilled large holes through metal bulkheads in order to allow a free flow of water. It took forty minutes before the British Navy became aware that German ships all around Scapa Flow were gradually sinking beneath its dark, cold waters.

Quick action by some British sailors prevented the sinking of some ships, but, one by one, fifty-two German ships gradually disappeared below the sea. One witness, who was ten years old at the time, later recalled, "During that time we watched the marvellous display as the German ships sank all around us. I counted them, twelve capital ships going down. Some sank by the bows and others by the stern and some stood right up in the water. It really was a marvellous display. In a way it was a very sad sight to see all these men getting into their boats; you really wondered what would happen to them. They had lost all their possessions. The whole thing was done in such a peaceful way. It was just the air escaping from the ships as they went down that caused the turbulence on the sea."

The first ship to sink, shortly after noon, was *Friedrich der Grosse*, and the last to sink, at around 5:00 pm that afternoon, was the battleship *Hindenburg* which remained upright in shallow water with its decks awash, and its funnels and superstructure clear of the water. The wreck of *Hindenburg* was to remain a familiar sight in the Flow for the next few years.

German Battleship Hindenburg lies in Scapa Flow

The remnants of the German fleet remained on the seabed of Scapa Flow as it was considered totally impractical and far too expensive to try to raise them. However, in 1924, salvage expert Edward Cox paid the British Admiralty the grand sum of £250 to purchase twenty-six destroyers and two battlecruisers. He then set about raising these ships from the seabed. This task took him over eight years to complete, and he added five battleships to his initial purchase. As each ship was raised, it was towed down the east coast of Scotland to the Firth of Forth where it was broken up for scrap metal, which was sold for profit. Edward Cox became known as the man who purchased a Navy!

The Bible states that every believer in the Lord Jesus has been bought with a price, *'Know ye not that your body is the temple of the Holy Ghost which is in you, which ye have of God, and ye are not your own? For ye are bought with a price: therefore glorify God in your body, and in your spirit, which are God's'* (1st Corinthians ch6v19&20). As we now belong to God, we cannot just do what we like. In any part of our Christian life we must seek only to do those things that please the Lord. When we were saved by trusting Christ, we handed ourselves over to God, and therefore must be obedient to all He asks us to do.

Flocks and Rocks

The Orkney coastline is unique. Some areas have beautiful sandy beaches, but elsewhere there are massive cliffs which tower many hundreds of feet above the restless waves which crash at their base. These majestic and breathtaking cliffs have become home to a huge variety of seabirds which build their nests high up in the various cracks and indentations of the rock face. It is from these cliffs that you will be able to observe the lovely kittiwake (kittick to Orcadians), its wings outstretched as it glides effortlessly along the air thermals. The less-attractive fulmar (malliemak to Orcadians) with its tubular-shaped beak will also float with fixed wings through the air. However, this master of the skies has a nasty surprise for anyone or anything that comes too close to its nest. It spits out a very nasty-smelling and sticky substance from its beak that is almost impossible to eradicate. The fulmar is now common around the rugged coastline even though it is a relative newcomer to Orkney, having not been seen prior to the early 1900s. Also making their homes along the Orkney coastline are guillemots (skout), razorbills (cooter-neb), puffins (sea coulter), and that largest British seabird, the hungry gannet (sula). A closer look at the gannet will reveal a most beautiful and streamlined head and body. Its yellow back and black wingtips make it easy to distinguish from most other seabirds. Its fishing trips are spectacular as it almost stops in flight, folds its wings back into its body and dives at great speed out of the sky, disappearing into the water below with a slight splash. Once in the sea, it literally flies through the water, its great wings becoming the equivalent of flippers as they help to propel it towards its prey.

There are lots of cliffs around the many islands, and over the process of time the continual pounding and power of the sea has carved some of them into unique shapes and impressive forms. Here are just a few to look out for.

The Vat of Kirbister. This is perhaps the best example in the islands of a rock arch. It is part of what the locals call a 'gloup', usually known as a sea jet or blowhole. This is where the sea forces water between rocks to shoot out like a pressurised fountain on the land. The Vat of Kirbister is on the northerly island of Stronsay and is actually large enough to manoeuvre a small boat through. A boat trip with an experienced local guide around Stronsay is most interesting as there are several tidal caves that can be entered by boat and enjoyed by the more enthusiastic adventurer.

Another natural stone arch is **Hole O' Row** along the Sandwick cliffs on the western Mainland. Situated on Row Head and clearly visible from the Bay of Skaill, Hole O' Row is a cave that has been broken through by the strong tides to form the current spectacular stone arch through which the sea plunges with incredible force during stormy weather.

On the Mainland, if you travel north-west from Stromness to pass Neban Point, then look out to sea from the cliffs, you will observe the impressive **North Gaulton Castle.** No, this is not a man-built castle to keep attacking armies away! It is a naturally-formed rock stack standing off the main cliffs and rising to a height of fifty-five metres. Today, it provides an exciting challenge to climbers brave enough to, firstly, attempt to reach it and, secondly, climb its treacherous cliff face.

Yesnaby Castle lies a little to the north of North Gaulton Castle and is in every way the latter's little brother. Once again, this rock stack requires great effort and determination to reach before you even commence to climb its twenty-five-metre cliff face. Yesnaby is worth seeing as it actually has a hole passing right through it just above its base which gives it the appearance of actually standing on two legs!

The Old Man of Hoy is perhaps Orkney's most famous rock or landmark. This wonderful sea stack, standing 137 metres in height, almost seems to guard the seaway into Hoy Sound and the entrance to Stromness Harbour. The stack is not mentioned in histories or recorded on maps before 1750, hence it appears to have been formed within the past 250 years. Like Yesnaby, the Old Man originally had two legs, but the rear leg collapsed into the sea some time in the late 1800s. The stack was first climbed in 1966 by famous mountaineer Sir Chris Bonnington and two others, however, many climbers attempt

The Old Man of Hoy

the long and dangerous ascent each year. In 2013, three men climbed the stack and performed the first BASE jump from it. Base jumping is where someone jumps from a tall **B**uilding, **A**ntenna, bridge (**S**pan) or a cliff (**E**arth), and then almost immediately releases a parachute in order to land safely. Sadly, one of the three men who successfully negotiated both climbing and jumping from the Old Man died less than two weeks later attempting another BASE jump in Switzerland. Geologists suggest that the remaining landmark stack has limited time and will eventually collapse and disappear into the sea. Until that time, however, the Old Man still attracts visitors and climbers eager to see and scale this impressive sandstone structure.

Many times throughout the Bible, God is described as a rock, someone who is totally dependable and will never let you down. The writer of Psalm 18 confidently states, *'The Lord is my rock, and my fortress, and my deliverer; my God, my strength, in whom I will trust; my buckler, and the horn of my salvation, and my high tower'* (Psalm 18v2). This is a wonderful picture of how great our God really is. Sometimes we talk about something being rock solid, and, using this term, we mean that it is absolutely trustworthy and fully dependable. That is what God is like! The believer in the Lord Jesus can speak to God about every problem, worry or concern that they have, knowing that God will be able to help them through any difficulties they are experiencing.

Blinded by a Blizzard

Have you ever been out without a light on a night that was so dark that you were unable to see where you were going? If you have, you will be able to imagine in some way what it would be like to be on a ship in total darkness in the middle of a great storm and during a snow blizzard. These were the conditions that met HMS *Opal* and HMS *Narborough* as they sought to return to the safety of Scapa Flow on the night of the 12th and early hours of the 13th January 1918.

Both destroyers had been out on patrol with a larger light cruiser, HMS *Boadicea*, searching for German ships laying mines around the Scottish coast. At 5:30 pm, due to the great storm, the captain of *Boadicea*, which was three times larger than the smaller vessels, ordered them back to port for fear that they would be overwhelmed by the severity of the worsening weather.

Both ships set course for Scapa Flow, HMS *Opal* sending regular wireless reports stating her progress and position. Four hours after leaving *Boadicea*, *Opal* suddenly sent a message, stating simply, 'Have run aground.' Silence followed, despite attempts being made to raise both *Opal* and *Narborough* by wireless. A search was commenced the next morning at first light, but it took two days to locate the wrecks of both *Opal* and *Narborough* off the east coast of South Ronaldsay. Amazingly, one man, William Sissons, survived the disaster by holding on to a ledge on a cliff for an agonising thirty-six hours before finally being rescued. Sadly, he was the only survivor, having seen 180 fellow sailors perish in the stormy sea.

When an investigation was conducted, it was determined that both ships had run straight into the cliffs of South Ronaldsay after making a navigational error, possibly as a result of the terrible storm.

Tragically, today millions of people are still going the wrong way and heading for the dreadful cliffs of eternal judgement. Many of these dear people are knocked off course by false religions or false promises of wealth and riches, when all the time the Lord Jesus stands offering eternal life to any who will trust Him. He came from Heaven, lived a perfect life and died in shame upon a cross in order to save your soul and bring you safely into Heaven. He says, '*I give unto them eternal life; and they shall never perish, neither shall any man pluck them out of my hand*' (John ch10v28). Thankfully, unlike poor William Sissons, we do not have to hold on to Christ. With His strong hand and powerful arm, He holds tightly to us once we have trusted Him as Saviour.

A Proper-Principled Politician

There is a funny statement that is often repeated when it comes to politics and politicians. It goes something like this – '99.9% of politicians give the rest a bad name!' This is simply stating that the majority of politicians are perceived by the public to be poor, bad, self-centred or just plain useless. Occasionally, though, a person enters parliament who, by their life and actions, is able to gain the respect, not only of their own political party, but also of those of other parties with a differing political outlook. One such man who gained this unusual respect was Orkney's Member of Parliament Jo Grimond.

Grimond entered Parliament in 1950 and was to remain the local MP for the Orkneys for a staggering thirty-three years before finally stepping down to retire in 1983. After his retirement he was hailed as 'the greatest politician never to become Prime Minister.'

In 1956, Grimond took over the leadership of the Liberal Party, a party that had almost been wiped off the political landscape of British politics in the general election the previous year. Some wondered if the party could indeed survive to fight another general election at all. Jo Grimond, however, had different ideas and plans. He was respected and trusted almost universally by all who knew him. He also possessed the gift of being able to argue a good case in public debate without resorting to attacking and belittling opponents. Someone wrote of him, 'He is a fluent speaker and can at times be vigorously eloquent and pleasantly humorous.' His gentlemanly manner and ability to work with all his colleagues resulted in him being able to modernise the Liberal Party and set a more forward-looking agenda than his predecessor. His charm and charisma paid off, and in the ten years he was at the helm of the Liberal Party he saw its number of MPs triple from three to nine. He also saw the party pulled back from the brink of extinction to become a force once again to be reckoned with in British politics. During his time as an MP, Jo Grimond returned to represent the islands in no less than ten general elections, often campaigning with the slogan 'Vote for Jo – the man you know.'

Voting Sign

When the Lord Jesus was dying on the cross, His enemies made a very startling confession in stating, 'He saved others' (Luke ch23v35). As they considered all that the Lord had done, they knew that He had changed people's lives. He was known for all that He claimed to be and all the wonderful things that He had done. The apostle Paul, speaking to King Agrippa, stated, 'This thing was not done in a corner' (Acts ch26v26). The work and ways of the Lord Jesus were well known during His life on earth and the results of his work in others is still seen today in changed lives, mended marriages, happy homes and altered destinies. It is well known what He can do, but have you allowed Him to save and change you?

Jo Grimond's marriage to his wife, Laura, lasted well over fifty years until his death at the age of eighty on 24th October 1993. This too was something of a record amongst British MPs, who seem to be so often linked to sleaze, smears and scandals, all of which Jo Grimond avoided. Having been the islands' MP for such a long time, and having gained the respect of so many during this period, his funeral service on 29th October was one of the largest the islands had seen, with hundreds packing into St Magnus Cathedral and then following the hearse to the Finstown Cemetery where Jo Grimond, 'the man who saved the Liberal party', was laid to rest.

The Crown of London

With a title such as this, you might expect that this chapter is going to be about the crown jewels, but you would be wrong! Instead, it is about a rebellion against the king who wore the crown.

In the early 1600s, the ruling Stuart family believed that they had power and authority given by God to rule the country. They called this belief 'the divine right of kings.' As a result of this, they were convinced that their position and power was above anything or anyone else. They further believed that it allowed them to dictate how services were conducted and even who was allowed to preach in churches.

In Scotland, many people left the established churches and began meeting in the open air to worship God. These people were called Covenanters, and their meetings were called conventicles. These actions resulted in the Established Church being given more power to persecute those who were not meeting in its services. The church's authority was supported by the use of troops who would break up conventicles, usually by force, arresting and often killing those attending. This resulted in almost a civil war in Scotland between those who conformed to the church and the king (doing what they were commanded) and those who were known as non-conformist (who wished to meet only in accordance with the Bible's instructions, without interference from the king or his church).

In 1679, 257 Covenanters, who had been captured at the Battle of Bothwell Bridge, were being transported as prisoners upon a ship called the Crown of London. They were being taken to America where they were to be sold as slaves. However, as the Crown of London anchored off Deerness on 10th December, its anchor cable broke in stormy weather and the ship was driven onto the rocks. The captain ordered all the hatches to be closed and locked so that none of his prisoners could escape, despite the fact that the ship was being broken up in the storm and was obviously going to sink. As the ship keeled over, the majority of the crew managed to escape along one of its masts that had formed a bridge to the land. Thankfully, one member of the crew risked his own life, and the wrath of his captain, by running through the ship, seeking to unlock hatches and doors to allow the Covenanters to escape. His brave actions resulted in forty-seven managing to flee the sinking ship and the seething sea, and making it safe to land. Unfortunately, the majority were soon rearrested and once more sent on their way to the slave grounds of America. There were some, though, who escaped and eventually settled to live in the Orkney Islands.

In 1888, a wealthy doctor named Robert Gunning gave £50 (a lot of money in those days) to pay for the erection of a memorial overlooking the site where the *Crown of London* foundered. Hundreds of people gathered to dedicate the memorial and remember those who died in the disaster. Two years later, a granite drinking fountain memorial

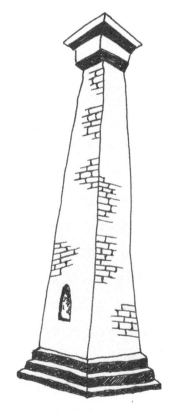

Covenanters' Memorial

was also put up in Kirkwall on Kirk Green. These two monuments stand today as reminders of Scotland's dark days and of those brave men and women who were prepared to sacrifice everything for what they believed to be right.

The inspiring stories from the times of the Covenanters should challenge us as to our love for the Lord and willingness to serve Him despite the cost. During that terrible period, soldiers were given orders which allowed them to kill at will anyone they suspected of belonging to the Covenanters' cause and, as a result, nearly twenty thousand people died for their faith. It was very costly to stand for what they believed in. The apostle Paul provides a great challenge to all Christians today – *'I beseech you therefore, brethren, by the mercies of God, that ye present your bodies a living sacrifice, holy, acceptable unto God, which is your reasonable service. And be not conformed to this world: but be ye transformed by the renewing of your mind, that ye may prove what is that good, and acceptable, and perfect, will of God'* (Romans ch12v1&2). It is not at all pleasant to be persecuted or ridiculed for what you believe, and none of us like it. There are still places in the world where it is illegal to be a Christian and to live for the Lord Jesus. No matter how hard it is, we still need to ensure that we place God right at the heart of our lives and seek always to live for Him. To help us do this, we have His wonderful promise, *'I will never leave thee, nor forsake thee'* (Hebrews ch13v5).

Gone but not Forgotten

Walking around a cemetery is always interesting, but also sobering, as we read the names and the inscriptions on the various headstones. A walk around the Naval Cemetery in Lyness on Hoy will certainly educate you greatly as there are various men of different ranks, ships, nationalities and regiments buried within the cemetery's walls.

Lyness Naval Cemetery

Nearly 450 servicemen from British and Commonwealth forces who perished during the First World War between 1915 and 1918, are buried here. As you read the inscriptions on the headstones, you will see that 107 have no name, as the bodies were unidentifiable at the time. Set apart in a little area by themselves are also the graves of thirteen German sailors who died between 1918 and 1919 during the German fleet's internment in Scapa Flow.

Among the ships that some of the sailors came from are HMS *Hampshire*, which sank off Marwick Head with Lord Kitchener on board, and HMS *Vanguard*, which blew up in Scapa Flow in 1917, killing all but two of her crew. A large stone monument was erected as a memorial to the 840 who died, most of whom still lie with their ship in the Flow. Also interned here are over fifty men from ships HMS *Narborough* and HMS *Opal*, which steamed into cliffs during a snowstorm in January 1918.

During the Second World War, the cemetery was once again used to bury those who had died on duty around the shores of Orkney. Around two hundred sailors, soldiers and airmen were buried at this time. Here lie twenty-six men from the battleship HMS *Royal Oak*, torpedoed by a German submarine at the start of the war.

If you look a little more closely at the headstones, you will notice that each has a symbol of the particular branch of the armed services in which the person buried there served. An anchor for the Royal Navy, a globe and laurel for the Royal Marines, the cannon and crown of the

Royal Artillery, the MN of the Merchant Navy, who were all civilians, and the eagle and crown of the Royal Air Force. So many individuals, from so many differing parts of the armed services, all joined together in order to fight oppression and evil, now lying together in Lyness cemetery on the windswept island of Hoy. This really is a place to stop and ponder the deeper realities of life.

As you wander around this sombre reminder of the cost of war, it is hard not to think of all the different men who lie beneath the well-kept lawns and flowerbeds. What sort of people were they? Some of those who could be identified were only teenagers who were prepared to give up everything so that their country would remain free. As we have stated, many came from different parts of the armed forces, but all were united in one common goal – the defeat of the enemy. Unity among Christians is important and stressed often, especially in the New Testament. When a person trusted the Lord Jesus in New Testament times, they were baptised by being fully immersed into water, which was a picture of the death, burial and resurrection of the Lord Jesus. Next, they joined a company of Christians who were seeking to obey the Lord in following His commands (see Acts ch2v41&42). Once they met with other believers they would want to work alongside them in serving God, *'Stand fast in one spirit, with one mind striving together for the faith of the gospel'* (Philippians ch1v27). If you are saved, you should seek to meet regularly with other Christians in order to learn with them and from them.

Sinking Ships and Remarkable Rescues

My father served in the Royal Navy during Word War Two. He often told me that the saddest sight he ever saw was a ship in its death throes as the sea finally claimed it, its cargo and often some of its crew. Several times he observed convoy ships that had been torpedoed sinking down to the ocean's depths. The last sight of a sinking ship, as its stern lifts high out of the water and then slips quickly out of sight in a mass of escaping air and grinding steel, must indeed leave a lasting impression on any watching such a sad and sorrowful sight.

The waters around the Orkney Islands are no strangers to shipwrecks, as we have already seen, and, sadly, thousands of people have died in the cold waters surrounding these exciting islands. In this chapter we would like to consider some of the lesser-known stories that have resulted in sinking ships and remarkable rescues.

Hope – When the Peterhead trawler *Hope* ran aground in the Holm of Faray during a storm on 28th December 1908, the nine-man crew would have known that they had little chance of survival. Faray is one of the smallest and least populated of the Orkney Islands, and as the storm continued to pound their small boat throughout the night, they might have concluded that *Hope* was in a hopeless situation.

However, early next morning, one of the local islanders, John Hercus, spotted the stranded trawler. He quickly realised the seriousness of the situation and gathered four others, including William Burgar who owned a thirteen-foot rowing boat. With great daring, the five men rowed their little boat across the storm-battered Lavey Sound to reach the stricken fishing boat. Their first trip rescued five of the crew, then they turned around and headed back through the storm and seething sea to repeat the feat by rescuing the remaining four.

Because of the severity of the storm, the island of Faray was cut off until 4th January and the rescued men were given food, clothes and beds in the houses of their rescuers. Once the news was made known about the daring rescue, letters of congratulations started to pour in from around the world, praising the islanders for their bravery. The men even made a trip to meet King Edward the 7th at his Scottish holiday home in Balmoral, and he presented them with a silver Board of Trade medal in recognition of their efforts.

Malta 2 – The *Malta* 2 was yet another fishing boat, that in 1911 met a sorrowful fate in the treacherous waters around Orkney. Strangely, however, this little boat provided an unusual warning of impending doom when some of its rats decided to leave when it called at Kirkwall. In sea folklore, rats are said to leave a ship when they sense danger is present. Two deckhands, upon seeing the fleeing rats, left the ship and refused to sail with it, their places being taken by two Orkney men. Not long after leaving Kirkwall, *Malta* 2 got into trouble and sank off the island of Auskerry. Thankfully, its crew were able to get into its lifeboats and were later picked up safe and sound by a passing small ship from Wick.

The Bible, God's Word, is full of warnings of one kind and another, each one placed in its pages to help guide us to God. John the Baptist, who was sent by God to initially point people to the Lord Jesus, asked the question, *'Who hath warned you to flee from the wrath to come?'* (Matthew ch3v7) Today we can answer this question by saying that God has warned us to flee to His Son, the Lord Jesus, in order to be saved from *'the wrath (judgement) to come.'* Just as the Bible tells us about Heaven, it also seriously warns about Hell as a place of never-ending torment for those who have rejected God's Son as their Saviour and have never turned from their sin. Thankfully, the Lord Jesus offers salvation and the assurance of Heaven forever to all who trust Him. The Bible records of others that they *'turned to God from idols to serve the living and true God; and to wait for His Son from Heaven, whom He raised from the dead, even Jesus, which delivered us from the wrath to come'* (1st Thessalonians ch1v9&10).

Johanna Thorden – The early hours of 12th January 1937 marked the beginning of what would become the largest peace-time loss of life in Orkney waters of the 20th century. The brand new Finnish motor vessel, the *Johanna Thorden*, was heading to Gothenburg in Sweden, having just completed her maiden voyage to New York.

As *Johanna Thorden* steamed past Orkney in a growing storm, she ran aground. Opinions differ as to where this took place, with some saying she hit Swona and others the Pentland Skerries. Unfortunately, the impact was so violent and sudden that it broke the wireless and transmitter, so the ship was unable to communicate with anyone or send an SOS message. The ship fired between thirty and forty rockets, which no one on the shore saw. The first lifeboat left the stranded ship at about 6:15 am, carrying twenty-five people, including women and children. Tragically, the boat never made it through the stormy seas as it capsized, throwing all who were aboard into the icy waters. A second lifeboat, carrying a further thirteen occupants, including the ship's captain, Lahja Simola, was launched an hour later and met a similar fate to the first boat, being overwhelmed by the mountainous waves. Despite being tipped into the sea, eight men from this lifeboat managed to swim and scramble ashore, and in doing so raised the alarm. Sadly, despite a large search and rescue operation, no other survivors were found, and twelve bodies were never recovered from the sea. Of the thirty-eight on board, thirty were lost and only eight saved!

The Johanna Thorden

The day an angel came to Westray – During a storm in 1730, a Russian ship was wrecked off the coast of Westray. Local islanders searched the seashore for survivors, but sadly found only the bodies of those who had died. As they turned over the body of a lady, they discovered a very young boy bound tightly to her breast, and even more amazing was the fact that he was still alive. He was quickly taken into a local home to be warmed up and given some food. Soon after this discovery, the name plate (or perhaps destination) of the ship was also washed ashore – Arkhangelsk – Archangel! The boy was therefore named Archie Angel and grew up with an adopted family on the island of Westray. The story continues that in 1760 he married a local girl called Jane Drever, and they had five children. In the 1841 census (a count of residents), there were fifteen people living on Westray with the surname Angel, all descendants of Archie, the sole survivor of the wrecked Archangel. The surname survived on the islands until the beginning of the 1900s.

The ship that blew up – Built in 1909 in Barrow-in-Furness, HMS *Vanguard* was a formidable battleship of her day. She weighed thirty thousand tons, measured over 160 metres in length, and had cost around 1.5 million pounds to build. *Vanguard* was an impressive sight during her regular visits to Scapa Flow.

At 11:20 pm on the night of 9th July 1917, a massive explosion suddenly tore through the ship, sending flame and metal parts hundreds of feet into the air. Much of this debris came crashing down onto the decks of nearby ships. When the smoke had cleared away, nothing was left on the surface of this once great ship. There were over eight hundred men on board *Vanguard* when she exploded, but tragically only three survived, one of these sadly dying soon after as a result of his injuries. The two survivors, Royal Marine J Williams and Stoker 1st Class F W Cox, explained that one moment they were asleep in their cabin and the next they were swimming in Scapa Flow among the wreckage that had once been their ship!

Midshipman R F Nicholls was not aboard *Vanguard* at the time of the explosion. He and some other members of the crew were attending a concert being held on board another ship. In 1939, Nicholls, now a commander, was on board HMS *Royal Oak* when it was torpedoed and sunk, also in Scapa Flow. Remarkably, he also survived that tragedy and eventually was promoted to captain and given command of his own ship.

An inquiry was set up which concluded that explosives stored on board had somehow detonated, causing other ammunition to do the same. The combined effect of tons of explosive all blowing up at the same time caused the almost instant destruction of the ship, resulting in the mass loss of life.

Feathers, Freedom and Fun

A visit to Orkney will be especially interesting if, like the author, you're a wildlife buff. While the seas around the islands are teaming with wildlife, Orkney's magnificent winged wonders are maybe of more interest. For those who are willing to seek them out, they are easily accessible. We considered a few in our chapter 'Rocks and Flocks' but there are many other exciting and rare birds that make Orkney their home for at least part of the year. In this chapter, we want to consider three of them and hopefully learn something special about these feathered marvels of God's creation.

The Arctic Tern – This amazing bird certainly holds the record for long distance flying, putting all other birds that migrate to different countries to shame. It usually measures between thirty and forty centimetres in length, with a pointed wingspan of somewhere around seventy centimetres. An Arctic tern will have a very distinctive and quite large black cap on its head, with a long, spear-like, deep red bill. Look out too for its deeply-forked tail, fairly short legs and webbed feet. It can often be seen almost hovering before diving steeply and quickly into the sea in search of its favourite food – sandeels.

The Arctic tern often nests on the cliffs of Rousay and Papay during the summer breeding season, usually laying two eggs, although laying three is not uncommon. If something comes too close to the nest, the parent birds will not hesitate to defend the nest by swooping low over the predator and giving it a hard blow with their sharp feet. This can easily cut a person's head if they happen to be unfortunate enough to be on the receiving end of such an attack. It will, however, usually cause any bird or animal to turn and flee, leaving the nest secure.

Once the chicks have been raised and can fend for themselves, the terns embark on a twenty-thousand-mile flight towards the Antarctic (bottom of the world) to spend the summer there. Once the Antarctic summer is over, the birds head back right to the top of the world. As a consequence, every year they fly in excess of forty thousand miles and sometimes as many as fifty thousand miles, migrating from the top to the bottom of the world, and experiencing the freedom of the skies. This all-action lifestyle must agree with them as Arctic terns are some of the most long-living birds in the world, their lives often exceeding twenty years!

Hen Harrier – One of the most impressive birds of prey that the author has ever seen is the beautiful hen harrier. With its great wingspan and a face looking like it is wearing spectacles, it is certainly a jaw-dropping sight when it suddenly rises up from the ground about twenty metres in front of you. The hen harrier stands around half a metre tall and has a wingspan of over twice its height. The female is nearly always heavily but uniformly streaked dark brown underneath on a light buff (stone) coloured background, making it distinctive amongst the birds of prey (raptors) of the British Isles. The male is a uniform light grey colour without the streaking, but has very distinctive black wingtips. Orkney certainly has its fair share of these wonderful birds, with well in excess of fifty nest sites recorded annually. Its favourite food is the Orkney vole, but it will take other things such as mice, small birds and even frogs. The hen harrier is most often seen sweeping low over hedgerows and ditches, looking for any movement that might signal its next meal.

Short-Eared Owl – Standing just short of half a metre in height and with a wingspan of about a metre, the short-eared owl is a pretty impressive-looking bird. If you are not a wise old owl yourself, and therefore not sure of the different British species, you could perhaps mistake the short-eared for a snowy owl as the author did on his first sighting! The streaking of the breast and wings gives it an almost white appearance that makes it stand out from the owl crowd. Its bright yellow eyes are surrounded by black circles that make it look like it is wearing a gangster-style mask. Its name comes from its two short feather tufts that can scarcely be seen protruding from the top of its head. These are not ears but just feathers that give the impression of ears. The short-eared owl is most easily spotted at dusk as it swoops low across fields, searching for voles and mice in the field margins.

Short-Eared Owl

In the Old Testament, God provided detailed restrictions on certain mammals and birds that His people could eat. Most of these laws are found in Leviticus chapter 11 and it would appear that there were certain characteristics in certain animals and birds that God did not want to see in His people. The owl is a killer of the night, seldom seen flying by day. God clearly instructs Christians to *'have no fellowship with the unfruitful works of darkness, but rather reprove them'* (Ephesians ch5v11). The Lord Jesus said, *'I am the light of the world: he that followeth Me shall not walk in darkness, but shall have the light of life'* (John ch8v12). The apostle Paul gave a command, *'For ye were sometimes darkness, but now are ye light in the Lord: walk as children of light'* (Ephesians ch5v8). As 'children of light' we should take great care to avoid anything that is dishonest, dirty or defiling in our lives – those things the Bible states are of the night. There are, however, good things that we can think on – *'Whatsoever things are true, whatsoever things are honest, whatsoever things are just, whatsoever things are pure, whatsoever things are lovely, whatsoever things are of good report; if there be any virtue, and if there be any praise, think on these things'* (Philippians ch4v8).

The Arctic Adventurer

I guess that most of us have heard about the so-called superheroes, whose adventures we can read about in books or maybe watch on TV. Well, in this chapter we are going to meet Orkney's own Superman – John Rae!

John was born in Orkney and was obviously clever as he decided to become a doctor. John left his home and headed south to Edinburgh to study medicine, eventually graduating from Edinburgh University as a doctor. Immediately after qualifying, Rae travelled to Canada and settled in the community of Moose Factory in Ontario, working as a surgeon for the Hudson's Bay Company. Adventure was never far from his thoughts and, whilst working, he designed his own snow shoes. He also learned the art of living off the land and began building up his stamina in order to travel great distances while only taking minimal supplies.

Whilst exploring the high Arctic areas of Canada in 1846, he became the first European to spend all winter in the high Arctic, learning how to build igloos in the process. He is reported to have stated that he found igloos much warmer to live in than tents. After this two-year adventure, Rae returned to Britain at the close of 1847.

In subsequent expeditions, John Rae surveyed and mapped over one thousand miles of frozen Arctic coastline. During his many adventures and expeditions, Rae learned, from the native Inuit and Cree Indians, how to survive the freezing temperatures and harsh weather conditions.

During 1845, a Royal Navy expedition set sail from Britain to try to discover what became known as the North West Passage which

Compass

connects the Pacific Ocean with the Atlantic Ocean through the use of the Arctic Ocean. This was led by the experienced rear admiral, Sir John Franklin, who commanded a crew of 134 men. However, in 1848, when nothing had been heard from the men or the two ships that sailed with him, a search operation was mounted that found no trace of the missing expedition.

In 1854, as Rae continued to explore the northern passageways of Arctic Canada, he discovered, with the help of the Inuit Indians, the remains of the Franklin expedition, and recovered various artefacts. To his surprise, Rae realised that some of Franklin's men had resorted to cannibalism (eating other humans) in order to stay alive. When Rae reported on his sad discovery, that all the men from the 1845 expedition were lost, it resulted in uproar in London. His findings of cannibalism were disbelieved and rejected as outright lies. John Franklin's widow obtained the help of influential friends, such as the famous author Charles Dickens, to discredit John Rae and his discoveries. Four years later, in 1859, even more evidence came to light, proving that John Rae was correct. However, the damage was done to his reputation as a great Arctic explorer, and whilst others were given awards and knighthoods, Rae was shunned and overlooked.

Perhaps Rae's greatest discovery was during 1854 when he found that the Arctic Ocean could indeed link the two greater oceans of the Pacific and the Atlantic through what was to become known as the Rae Straight. The elusive North West Passage had finally been discovered to be navigable.

When John Rae died in 1893 in London, his body was brought back to Kirkwall and laid to rest in the grounds of St Magnus Cathedral. An impressive memorial sculpture of Rae sleeping with his gun by his side was set up within the confines of St Rognvald's Chapel.

Do you love reading adventure stories? I know that I did, and I still do. In fact, I was named after the great Antarctic explorer, Captain Robert Scott. The Bible is just full of great stories of adventure of one sort or another, all of which make it such an exciting book. The greatest adventure, however, that anyone can embark on is that of walking with God. It commences when we get saved by trusting the Lord Jesus, and continues daily as we read the Bible and spend time in prayer. In Proverbs, we are instructed to *'trust in the Lord with all thine heart; and lean not unto thine own understanding. In all thy ways acknowledge Him* (God)*, and He shall direct thy paths'* (Proverbs ch3v5&6). During this adventure, as we are guided by God, we will discover new things about Him, the Lord Jesus, ourselves and the world on an almost daily basis, until at last we land on the wonderful eternal shores of Heaven.

Companion volume in the 'Discover Britain' series
by Robert Plant:

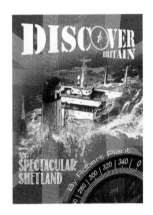

Spectacular Shetland
ISBN 9781910513170

Available from:

www.ritchiechristianmedia.co.uk

Books by

Robert Plant for ages 8-13:

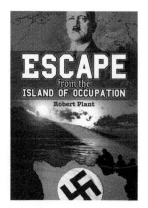

Escape from the Island of Occupation
ISBN 9781909803954

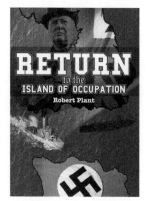

Return to the Island of Occupation
ISBN 9781910513484

Books by Ruth Chesney

for ages 10+ in the Search for Truth series

Book 1: Evidence
ISBN 9781910513361

Book 2: Witness
ISBN 9781910513620

Books by Ruth Chesney

for ages 3-6

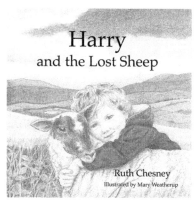

Harry and the Lost Sheep
ISBN 9781910513514

Harry and the Muddy Pig
ISBN 9781910513743